for

the world's greatest mom

from

for

the world's greatest mom

from

redeem this card for a
day of pampering
at:

for

the world's greatest mom

from

this card entitles you to
a very special

weekend getaway

to: _____

redeem this card for *three*

pick-up and deliveries

of your choosing

one:

two:

three:

this card entitles you to your own personal

garden assistant

for

the world's greatest mom

▲ ▶ ◀ from ▲ ◀ ▲

this card entitles you to
a day of complimentary,
full-service

laundry

➡ wash and fold
➡ delicates
➡ dry cleaning

for
the world's greatest mom
▲▶◀ from ▲◀◀

use this card for

_____

_____

this card entitles the holder
to one **absolute** **yes**
and
unconditional

redeem this card for
one week's personal

caffeine delivery

service

your order:

bath/shower

toilet

this card entitles you to

a sparkling-clean bathroom

floor

sink

use this card
for a
picnic
in the
park

redeem for
one full week of daily
super-duper
extra-
thorough

dish duty

mon · tues · wed · thurs · fri · sat · sun

for
the world's greatest mom
from

this card is good
for one free

_____

_____

_____

this card entitles the holder to
a day at the
beach

for

the world's greatest mom

from

this card entitles you to

wine and dine

at chez nous

for
the world's greatest mom
▲ ▶ ◀ from ▲ ◀ ▲

redeem for a day of

beauty

 nails:

hair:

makeup:

for
the world's greatest mom
▲▶◀ from ▲◀◀

for
the world's greatest mom
▲▶▲ from ▲◀▲